HELPING YOUR TEEN MAKE HEALTHY CHOICES

About Dating and Intimacy

— A Life Guide —

HELPING YOUR TEEN MAKE HEALTHY CHOICES

About Dating and Intimacy

— A Life Guide —

Dr. Suzanne Gelb, PhD, JD

FIRST EDITION

All rights reserved. This book or any portion thereof may not be reproduced or used in any manner whatsoever without the express written permission of the publisher except for the use of brief quotations in a book review.

Copyright © 2019 Dr. Suzanne J. Gelb, Ph.D., J.D.

Manufactured in the United States of America.

ISBN-13: 978-1-950764-07-5
ISBN-10: 1-950764-07-9

www.DrSuzanneGelb.com

CONTENTS

Disclaimer.   xi

INTRODUCTION.

Help Your Teen To Make Healthy Choices, Help Your Teen To Live a Happy, Well-Adjusted Life.   1

WHAT'S INSIDE AND HOW TO USE THIS GUIDE.   5

SAFETY PRACTICE #1.

Supervise Dating.   6

SAFETY PRACTICE #2.

Enforce Consequences.   12

SAFETY PRACTICE #3.

Ensure Online Safety.   17

SAFETY PRACTICE #4.

Give Appropriate Choices.   21

SAFETY PRACTICE #5.

Teach the Power of "No."   24

SAFETY PRACTICE #6.

Educate!   29

SAFETY PRACTICE #7.

Lead by Example.   33

A FEW FINAL WORDS.

Making a Difference.   36

MORE TIPS, MORE TOOLS.

4 FAQs About Tricky Parenting Challenges With Teens.   38

WHAT'S NEXT.

Resources… To Keep Navigating the Teen Years With Confidence.   85

ABOUT THE AUTHOR.   94

OTHER BOOKS BY THE AUTHOR.   95

INDEX.   97

DISCLAIMER

This book is a tool that can help you to help your teen make healthy, age-appropriate choices about dating and intimacy

This book contains educational exercises and tips drawn from my career in the field of emotional wellness with over 30 years of experience. This book is for informational purposes only, and is not intended to diagnose or treat any illness, nor is it a substitute for professional or psychological advice, diagnosis, or treatment. Always consult a qualified health care professional before engaging in any new, self-help resource (such as this one) and with questions you may have about your health and wellbeing.

Any case material that may be alluded to in this book, including in articles, or in interviews [see Resources section] does not constitute guarantees of similar outcomes for the reader. No results can be promised, since everyone's personal development path is unique. Names and details have been changed for privacy.

Links inside this book to external websites are for informational purposes only. Linking does not imply endorsement of or affiliation with that site, its content, or any product or service it may offer.

All link URLs in this book are current at the time of printing. Link URLs may fail at some point if the page has been deleted or moved. The author assumes no responsibility or liability for broken links.

This concludes the disclaimer portion of this book.

Thank you. Enjoy this Guide ... and enjoy your life.

INTRODUCTION

Help Your Teen To Make Healthy Choices, Help Your Teen To Live a Happy, Well-Adjusted Life

Welcome to The Life Guide on Helping Your Teen Make Healthy Choices about Dating and Intimacy.[1]

If you picked up a copy of this Guide, chances are, you might be feeling ...

— **Worried.**

("My teenage daughter wants to date a much older boy. I'm worried this could turn out very badly...")

— **Frustrated.**

---

[1] In this Life Guide "Intimacy" and "Sex" are used interchangeably.

("I've tried to set guidelines — like having a 9 pm curfew on school nights — but my son won't listen. He's out with his friends, and girls, doing God knows what.")

— **Guilty**.

("I should have had The Talk with my teenager years ago. I didn't know how to talk to my kid about dating + sex, and now I'm afraid it's too late.")

— **Hypocritical**.

("I don't want my child to make the same choices that I did — but since I was dating and having sex when I was 15, what right do I have to tell her, otherwise?")

— **Hopeless**.

("Honestly, my teenager is probably already having sex. I just pray he's using a condom ... I don't know what I can do to help, at this point. He doesn't listen.")

You're not alone.

Many parents feel uncertain about how to help their teens make healthy choices about dating and intimacy (sex).

Many wait until **the last possible moment**, and then try to pack every single lesson about dating, sex and respecting your body into one conversation — **"The Talk."**

But educating your child about sex doesn't happen in the course of one conversation.

In an ideal world, you would have been preparing your child since early childhood —

- Through a series of **age-appropriate conversations** ...

- Teaching your child t**he value of "No"**...

and by

- Modeling what it looks like to take loving, respectful care of your body.

The unfortunate reality is, by the time your child is a **teenager**, **it's much harder to "get through" to them**.

You just **don't have the same level of influence** over their decisions, anymore.

It can often feel as though you are slogging through an uphill battle.

But that doesn't mean you shouldn't **try to do what is right — for them**.

It may be more difficult, now, but it's never too late.

This Life Guide can help.

You can think of this Life Guide as **a "last chance guidebook"** — **a series of 7 safety practices** that you can use to **help your teen make healthy choices about dating and sex**, while they are still living under your roof.

Some of the safety practices in this guide may feel "too harsh" or "controlling," especially if you've been quite lax about setting rules and enforcing consequences in the past.

You may find yourself thinking,

"If I say this — or do that — my teenager will never speak to me again!"

But remember: as a parent, **your job is not to be your teenager's "friend."**

Your job is to be a parent.

Which means …

— Giving your child every possible chance to live a happy, well-adjusted life.

And

— Taking steps to ensure that your child doesn't engage in risky sexual behavior that could affect his (or her) physical and emotional wellbeing.

You **can** do this — and if you reflect on this situation for a moment… you may very well conclude that you **need** to do this.

Let's begin.

What's Inside and How To Use This Guide

Inside this **Life Guide**, you'll find a series of 7 safety practices to help your teen make healthy, age-appropriate choices about dating and sex.

For the purposes of this Life Guide, "teens" are defined as "youths ages 13 - 17," although nowadays kids as young as 10 are dating.

The Contents page of the book gave you a peek at what's ahead.

SAFETY PRACTICE #1.

Supervise Dating

"Our 15-year-old wants to date an 18-year-old boy. What do we do?"

"My 14-year-old sneaks out to date older boys. How do I stop her?"

"My 16-year-old keeps going to the mall with her friends after school. She says they're just 'hanging out,' but I think there's a boy in the group that she likes ... who knows what they're up to?"

These are real concerns from real parents who have stepped into my office.

I empathize with them, deeply.

For a parent, not knowing what your teenager is "up to" is a nerve-wracking experience.

But the solution is simple.

Start knowing.

Meaning:

Start **supervising** your teenager's dates.

Supervised dating may seem like a relic from the 1950s — conjuring up images of soda fountains and poodle skirts. But it's not "silly" or "out of date."

Supervised dating can offer teens **positive social experiences** that prepare them for **healthy relationships in adulthood**.

Why supervise?

It's natural for teens to be curious about dating and to want to experience it. It's up to you, as a parent, to ensure that these encounters are safe.

Curiosity, hormones, peer pressure, the media and **the Internet** can influence even the "smartest" teen to make poor choices such as premature sex, drug experimentation and drinking.

A discussion with your teen is **not likely to completely curb curiosity and hormones** that are active during dating — but **supervision will.**

How to supervise a date.

It's pretty simple:

Be there. The whole time.

You can allow your teen to have a 1:1 date, or you can encourage them to go on a group date with several friends.

You can give your teen **a little "space"** (for example, sitting a few rows back in the movie theater, rather than right next to him) but you should **be presen**t the entire time.

Start things off by saying to your teen:

"It's perfectly OK if you want to go on a date with [name].

But because I care about you, I'm going to be there to supervise."

If your teen whines or complains, say:

"This is not up for negotiation.

If you want to have this date, I will be there to supervise.

Now, what would be fun for you two to do?"

Hold firm, even if your teenager gets angry.

Remember: you're a parent, not a buddy.

This is your job.

If your teen says,

"But you never supervised my dates, before! Why now?"

You can say:

"You're right — I have not supervised your dates, before, and that was my mistake.

It's my job to keep you safe, and to help you make choices that will set you up for a healthy, happy future. By being absent from your dates in the past, I let you down.

But that won't happen again."

If your teenager continues to **whine or complain**, say:

"This is not up for negotiation.

If you want to have this date, I will be there to supervise.

Now, what would be fun for you two to do?"

Here are a few examples of supervised dates:

— Taking your teenage daughter and her date to the movies, and sitting close by, or one or two rows behind them.

— Taking your teenage son and his date, and a group of friends to the mall, and reading a book while they get lunch, hold hands and chat.

— Doing an outdoor activity together, as a family — like hiking or bicycling, canoeing or gardening — and encouraging your teenage daughter to invite her boyfriend to join in.

— Taking your teenage son to a park, and allowing him to enjoy a romantic picnic with his girlfriend, while you read a book on a bench a little ways away, out of earshot.

— Allowing your teenage son and his girlfriend to sit close together on the couch at home, watching TV, while you prepare dinner in the kitchen.

— Allowing your older teen daughter to spend alone time in her bedroom with her boyfriend, but keeping the door propped open the whole time.

No matter where you are (or what you're doing), the message should be clear:

"Make good choices. I'm right here."

In time, if your teenager demonstrates that he (or she) is capable of making good choices, consistently, you may decide to be a little more "lenient" with your supervision.

- Maybe you'll sit outside of the restaurant reading a book, instead of right at the next table.

Or

- Maybe you'll be inside the mall while your teen and her date explore a bookstore, but not right by their side.

Use **sound judgement** to decide how much supervision is necessary, but always **err on the side of caution**. All it takes is one slip-up to lead to an unplanned pregnancy, or some other consequence that could derail your child's entire life.

Of course, even with excellent supervision, some teenagers will try to "bend the rules" and go on a date without you — or engage in some other form of risky behavior.

If that happens, it's up to you to **enforce consequences** — which is what we'll cover in Safety Practice #2.

SAFETY PRACTICE # 2

Enforce Consequences

"My daughter promised that she wouldn't date Mike without supervision.

But last night, she snuck out of the house after bedtime.

I know she went to see him.

Now what?"

Teenagers must learn to consider the **consequences** of their choices.

In this example, the teenage daughter needs to be aware that sneaking out could put her in harm's way — and cause her to be grounded.

Enforcing consequences is an essential safety practice. If you **give in** or are **inconsistent** with your enforcement, your teen will quickly learn not to take you seriously — and that is a very dangerous situation.

But before you enforce "the rules," you need to make sure your teen understands what "the rules" are.

Have a conversation with your teenager, and say:

"I know that you are interested in dating.

I'm excited for you, and I'm going to set some ground rules.

*I'm doing this because **I care about you**, and because as your parent, it's my job to **make sure you're always safe**."*

The two most important rules are:

1. Until I say otherwise, all of your dates are going to be supervised by me or another trusted adult. Going on a date without this supervision is not allowed.

2. If you are going to a party or a sleepover at someone's house, I will need to speak to the other child's parents, first. I'll need you to give me their phone number, so that I can check in with them.

If you go on a date without being supervised, or attend a party without giving me the other parents' contact information, there will be serious consequences —

You will be grounded for two weeks.

That means your cell phone and laptop will be taken away, you will not be allowed to socialize with your friends, and you will not be allowed to go on dates, even with supervision. Do you understand?"

[Have your teen **verbally confirm** that they understand.]

"Good. You may think that these rules are harsh, but as your parent, it's my job to ensure that you are safe. That's my #1 priority. I want to prepare you for a happy, healthy adulthood, and this is how I'm going to do that."

If you're having this conversation with your teen a bit "late in the game," you may wish to apologize to your teen by saying:

"This is a conversation that I should have had with you, months ago. That was my responsibility, and I let you down.

I apologize for that. It will not happen again."

Choosing the right consequence.

"Grounding" is a commonly-used consequence — and it's a good one when the rule-breaking warrants it.

But use common sense — if "grounding" is unlikely to deter your teen, choose a different consequence — one that will cause your child to think,

"No, I don't want that to happen."

Perhaps not allowing your daughter to compete in a dance competition that she's been training for would be a better consequence — or revoking your son's privilege to use the family car.

Whatever consequence you choose, make sure it's appropriate (not too severe, but not too lax), communicated clearly — and enforced consistently.

Tracking your teen.

There are so many ways to track your teen's whereabouts and make sure that they are following your rules.

Just do an internet search with search terms like, "apps to track my teen" or something similar, and you're likely to find quite a few options.

One good option is **TeenSafe.**

This is an iPhone app that allows you to view your teen's phone calls, text messages (even deleted text messages), monitor your teen's location with GPS, and more.

You can get a free trial at TeenSafe.com.

Kitestring is another amazing app — not just for teens who are dating, but for people of all ages.

If you're going out on a first date — or meeting up with someone you don't know very well — send a text message to Kitestring.

Later, Kitestring checks up on you with a text message. Reply to the message to check in and indicate that you're safe. If you don't check in, Kitestring sends your emergency contacts a personalized alert message. It's free to use.

Get started at http://Kitestring.io.

Technology can be a powerful ally in your efforts to keep your teen safe. But when used inappropriately, it can also be a hazard.

That is what we'll talk about in Safety Practice #3: Ensure online safety.

SAFETY PRACTICE # 3

Ensure Online Safety

Fourteen-year-old Ellie just came home from school. A quiet girl, without many close friends at her new school, she's feeling **lonely** because she doesn't have a boyfriend.

Ellie logs onto an online dating site, and lies about her birthdate so that she can start an account.

She uploads a few photos and within minutes, she receives a message:

"Great photo, you're cute. Let's talk or meet, we have lots in common."

Ellie feels a surge of **excitement, receiving this attention** from a man who claims to be 18 — just a few years older than her. This guy doesn't know that she's **not popular at school**.

Online, she can create a new "persona" and be whoever she wants to be ...

Scenarios like these are all-too-common, and **simply having a conversation with your teen about the dangers of online dating isn't enough**.

Like we've discussed earlier in this Life Guide: "conversations" rarely influence teenager's decisions. Supervision, rules and consequences do.

Keep your teen safe.

Using **online dating sites** is a perfectly healthy way to connect with new people and find dates — when you're at an **appropriate age**.

But until your teenager is at least 18 years old, it's not a safe place to be.

To keep your teen safe, online, follow these simple guidelines:

Supervise.

Review.

Educate.

Block.

Supervise online activity — with a tracking app, and / or by situating the family computer in a public area, like the living room.

Nearly 30% of teens have been contacted by a total stranger, online. Supervision is not a joke!

- **Review your teenager's social media profiles** (Facebook, Twitter, Instagram, Pinterest).

If you see something **troubling** (like scantily clad photos of your teenage daughter at a college party), it's time to **set some new rules — and consequences**.

- **Educate** your teen about the **dangers of posting sensitive information online** — like your address, telephone number or last name.

- **Emphasize** that information that's posted online is **trackable, forever** — even if you delete it.

    Tools like the Wayback Machine mean that even deleted info can be recovered, by people who really want to find it.)

www.wayback.com/

Block certain sites (like porn sites, adult chat rooms, and online dating sites) so that your teen cannot access them, period.

SafeGuard is a popular **site-blocking tool**.

https://bit.ly/2NIJ3Zr

If you're unclear about how to block sites, find a friendly geek who can help.

So far, in this Life Guide, we've placed a lot of emphasis on **supervision**.

Supervision is important, but it's also important to give your teen the ability to make his or her own choices — within your parameters.

Giving your teen the **opportunity to make choices** prepares him (or her) for the **future**, when they're old enough to not need a parent to be around, to **make the final call**.

That's what we'll cover in Safety Practice #4: Give appropriate choices.

SAFETY PRACTICE # 4

Give Appropriate Choices

One reason **teenagers rebel and "bend the rules,"** is because they feel that all their power has been stripped away.

In response, **they resist conforming**.

Your job, as a parent, includes setting rules and enforcing consequences where necessary ... and also giving your teen opportunities to make his (or her) own choices.

One of the best ways to do this is to offer two "parent-approved" options, and then invite your teen to choose the one that he (or she) prefers.

For example:

— *"Yes, you can go on a date with Kendra, and I'll be happy to supervise you.*

Would you like to go to the park, or head to the movies?"

— *"Yes, you can invite Kevin to come over after school. Would you like to watch a movie together in the living room, or hang out in your bedroom, with the door propped open?"*

— *"Yes, you can go to Sasha's sleepover party, as long as you finish your chores before you go.*

And thank you for giving me her parents' phone number, so I can check in.

Will you be taking care of your chores right now, before your dance class, or first thing tomorrow morning?"

— *"That's great that Greg's parents have invited you to join their family on a summer camping trip.*

How would you like to say 'thank you'? With a handwritten card? Or do you want to bake some cookies for Greg's mom?"

By presenting your teen with two "good options," you're reinforcing sound morals and self-respect.

If your teen pushes back and says,

"Neither of those options sound good!"

You can invite them to propose a third option.

"Well, what sounds like a good option to you?"

But if your teen's suggestion is inappropriate, remember, it's your job to say:

"Nope, that option isn't appropriate. You can choose from one of the two that I just offered, instead."

As a parent, it can sometimes feel like you're saying "No" a million times a day. But that's not a necessarily a negative. "No" is a powerful word.

Each time you say it, you're:

- **Reinforcing clear boundaries**

And

- **Teaching your teen the right way to behave.**

In **Safety Practice #5**, we're going to continue exploring **the power of "No."**

SAFETY PRACTICE # 5

Teach the Power of "No"

"My daughter asked me if she can go on birth control, so I know she's about to start having sex — or maybe she already is.

I'm worried she's wanting to / or having sex for the wrong reasons.

She has struggled with self-esteem in the past ... now what?"

As an adult, you may find that it's hard to say "No."

— Maybe you struggle to say "No" when your boss asks you to work overtime.

— Maybe you struggle to say "No" when your brother or sister is asking for money to start up a "brilliant" new business (again).

Saying "No" can be uncomfortable — and if it's difficult for you, multiply that difficulty by about one thousand.

That's how difficult it can be for your teen to say "No" to sex when:

- hormones

- curiosity

- peer pressure

- loneliness

Or

- low self-esteem

are all part of the mix.

It's your job to impress upon your teen that it's OK to say "No" — and that "No" is a complete sentence.

Explain that saying "No" indicates that:

— you have a lot of **self-respect**

— you **care about yourself**, and want to stay **healthy** and **happy**.

Explain that:

— having contact with the opposite sex doesn't mean it has to be sexual.

— there are many ways to express affection:

Examples:

- Intimate talks

- Long walks

- Holding hands.

Explain that:

— many teens who decide to become sexual at a young age, later regret it.

One of my teen clients said it best,

"It wasn't worth it. I did it to get attention and be liked, but afterwards I felt bad.

I wish I had waited."

If you fear that your teen is struggling to say "No," you can break the ice by apologizing.

"I know that the idea of having sex can feel very exciting, but sometimes, we feel compelled to have sex for the wrong reasons.

If you want to have to sex because you're lonely, bored, or think it will make people like you more, those are not the right reasons.

It's important to remember that you always have the right to say 'No.'

I'm sorry I didn't talk to you about this earlier.

I realize now I should've cautioned you that peer pressure and loneliness are poor reasons to have sex.

I hope you'll postpone sex until you've found that one-in-a-lifetime person with whom you want to spend the rest of your life.

That's my wish for you.

Until then, I hope that you'll say No."

Helping your teen to say "No" — especially in the face of peer pressure — is no easy feat.

But it's not a lost cause.

Keep reinforcing that saying "No" is a powerful form of self-respect.

Reinforce that you believe in your teen's ability to do what is right.

"Saying 'No' can be tough, but I believe in you.

Once you're older, and you've left the house, I won't always be around to supervise you.

But I know that when it comes down to it, you will make the right choices.

Because you're learning how to respect yourself, a lot."

In addition to teaching your teen the power of "No," it's important to make sure that your teen is fully informed about the emotional and physical health risks of sex, too.

You can't necessarily rely on your child's school to fill in all the gaps... no matter how good the education may be.

It's up to you to make sure that all of the information that you, specifically, want your child to be up to speed on, is conveyed.

Sex education is essentially, first and foremost, a parent's responsibility.

Why?

Because you are your child's most important teacher.

Your teaching can make the greatest impact on your child.

This is such a **privilege**... and a **responsibility**.

Exercise this privilege wisely.

Assume this responsibility whole-heartedly.

That's what we'll cover in Safety Practice #6.

SAFETY PRACTICE # 6

Educate!

"I sat down with my son to give him 'The Talk' about the birds and the bees.

He blushed beet red, and I could tell he was totally embarrassed and tuning me out.

I doubt he really listened to a single word I said."

Let's be honest: for many teenagers, the LAST person on earth that they want to learn about sex from ... is their mom or dad.

But no matter how awkward it may feel, as a parent, educating your teen about sex is still YOUR responsibility.

To ease the tension, and make sure that your message really sinks in, give your teen books, videos and other tools that they can explore on their own.

It's important that the resources that you give to your child, reflect your personal views on this subject. So take your time as you look into what would be best to share with your child, and gather these materials.

You might already have some resources, based on prior reading and / or self-educating. If you want to further build your research list, or if you're starting from scratch, you could begin with an internet search for websites and books, or possibly visit your local library.

You can still be an educator, without literally pulling out a clipboard and doing all the teaching / education, yourself.

Fast forward a bit....

You're ready (well, as ready as you can be!) to broach "this subject" with your child. But suddenly you feel tongue-tied, and think to yourself,

"I don't know where to begin...

I'm never at a loss for words, especially with my child.

But now?

I'm stuck.

I'm speechless.

But I know I need to need this.

Ugh! How to I get this talk going?"

Here's one way to kick off the conversation.

"[Your child's name], you're at an age where you might be starting to feel curious about dating and sex.

Maybe you're very curious, already.

I remember what it felt like when I was your age.

I wish that somebody had given me the information I needed back then, to really understand what was happening in my body, and to fully understand the beauty and the purpose of sex, and how unwise it is to have sex prematurely.

If you have any questions about your body, or about sex, I am always here to help you.

I hope you'll always feel comfortable coming to me with your questions.

But in the meantime, I want to give you some books and resources that you can explore on your own."

At this point, you would offer the resources that you've previously gathered, to your teen.

Quick recap.

So far, we've talked about the importance of,

- supervision

- setting rules

- enforcing consequences

and

- educating your teen about the physical and emotional realities of sex.

But none of those Safety Practices will "stick" if you don't model the lessons that you teach.

(Teenagers have very finely-tuned "hypocrisy radar" — as you probably remember, from back when you were a teen!)

In our final Safety Practice, we'll talk about **how to lead by example**.

SAFETY PRACTICE # 7

Lead by example

If you haven't watched this powerful video — created by a child abuse prevention organization in Australia — take a moment to watch it.

https://bit.ly/2xYvwXr

The message is harrowing, but true.

"Children see. Children do."

The best way to teach your teenager about what it means to make good, sensible, self-respecting choices ... is to make those kinds of choices, yourself.

If you frequently cave under pressure and **say "Yes" when you mean "No"** ...

then that's what your child will learn to do, too.

If you're a single parent who is dating, and you rush into sex — bringing home dates too quickly, because you're desperate to feel desired —

then that's what your child will learn to do, too.

If you constantly speak critically about your body, or treat your body in a disrespectful way,

then that's what your child will learn to do, too.

But if you **show your child what it means to be a**

- safe

- sensible

and

- self- respecting decision-maker…

- leading by example, every day —

then that's what your child will learn to do, too.

It's not complicated. It is simple. And it is your job.

And no matter how you were raised, or the kind of "example" that your parents set — or didn't set — you can choose to do better. Starting now.

A gentle note:

If you find yourself having a hard time with leading by example, because you can't seem to change certain patterns on your own, please seek professional help.

Do it for yourself, and for your child's sake, as well. Find a qualified healthcare provider, near you.

A FEW FINAL WORDS

Making a difference

Until the end of history as we know it, teenagers are always going to be curious about dating and sex.

You were.

I was.

There's no denying that reality.

But even if it seems like it's "just too late" to "get through" to your teenager — it's not.

It may be difficult to help your teen make good choices about dating and sex, but it's not impossible.

By

- supervising your teen

- setting age-appropriate rules

- enforcing consequences consistently

- teaching the power of "No"

and

- modeling what it looks like to take good, self-respecting care of your body and mind

you CAN make a difference.

Your teenager might not "like" it, but once again, your job isn't to be "liked."

Your job is to do what is right — and to set your teen up for a happy, healthy, well-adjusted life.

You can do it.

And hopefully one day?

Your teen will be **very grateful** that you did.

MORE TIPS, MORE TOOLS

FAQs About Tricky Parenting Challenges

Ready for even more tips and tools to continue your journey to set your teen up to make healthy decisions that can set him or her up for a great life?

Read on for my answers[2] to some of the more typical questions that I've been have asked over the past 3+ decades by parents who wanted to learn how to best parent their teens, especially when it comes to dating and sex.

Enjoy!

---

[2] The questions and answers are summarized here, to maximize your learning experience.

Question No. 1 — It's Just a Phase

Realizing That "He Won't Just Grow Out of It"

My son is 13 and he is smitten by a girl. She's all he thinks about and talks about.

When I see him day-dreaming while his he doing his homework, and I ask him what's on this mind, he always says:

"This girl I'm in love with. She's the one! One day, I'll marry her."

His dad and I laugh it off as, "Just a phase is going through" and "his hormones will calm down and then he'll come to his senses" [he ends up getting his homework done, by the way.]

But now I'm worrying that he may be sexually active because some subtle signs catch my attention — little things he says and does. I don't want my son to be having sex at his age. But I'm wondering if I can disregard my worries, by telling myself, "It's just puppy love, he'll grow out of it."

I don't know if I'm being overbearing... maybe too overprotective, and if I should trust him more, and believe that he'll be fine.

But we've never talked about the birds and the bees, so I don't know how much he knows or doesn't... or what he's learned from his friends.

I avoid talking to my son about this, and his dad won't touch it.

I'd prefer to let this phase play itself out, and talk to my son about all of this when he's older, but is that risky?

Response:

I'd be wary of the "he'll grow out of it" attitude.

Generally, teens don't "grow out of it" - one poor choice tends to often lead to another, especially when:

- There's peer pressure

and

- Older children entice younger ones to give in to their curiosity and try to gain approval by trying things like sex.

Yes, in time hormones settle, but the basic ignorance (lack of information / understanding) about one's body, sexual drive, intimacy, etc., remains... and needs to be addressed.

Otherwise, poor decision-making and risky choices because of ignorance, may very well follow.

Generally, teens don't "grow out of it" - one poor choice leads to another, especially when there's peer pressure, and older children entice younger ones to indulge their curiosity and seek

It Must Be Love...

As for your 13-year-old thinking that he's in love with a girl, here are some good question to ask yourself:

"Knowing my son as well as I do, do I think he is emotionally mature enough to truly know love?

Do I think he is experienced enough, at age 13, to be able to determine that what he is experiencing is true love?

Do I think that my son is mature enough to be able to arrive at the beautiful, but incredibly significant conclusion that "This is the one. My partner for life?"

If your answer to any of the three questions above is "No," then now's a good time for you to take a deep breath, so you can then "reach" within yourself and find the courage to have a talk with your son, so that you can educate him about crushes and love feelings and sex.

Based on what you shared on your question, a simple way to approach this with your son, might be a brief conversation (for starters) that goes something like this:

"I understand that you feel like you're in love, and I'm happy that you're enjoying these feelings.

And I want you to know that having a crush on someone, and the love feelings that go along with this, are natural, but...

Sex is something entirely different and separate.

Sex is something that should occur when you are an adult, with more experience and maturity behind you, and when you are in a relationship that is based on love and commitment."

You can then ask your son if he has any questions. If he says "No," let that be ok. Don't belabor the point or press him for a response to what you just shared.

As long as you share what's in your mind with your son,

• In a Calm Way,

- **Without Sounding Accusatory, or**

- **Using a Tone That Is Critical or Judgemental,**

then, you've created an opportunity for him to think about something that's **very important** to his **physical and emotional wellbeing**.

For that you can be proud.

Follow-Up Question

Deciding When To Have "the Talk."

What if I'm wrong, and my son isn't having sex or even thinking about having sex, and here I am talking to him about waiting to have sex.

Is my bringing up the topic of sex with my son going to make him want to experiment?

At the same time, like I said in my first question, I've seen some signs that make me suspicious that my son might be doing more than just holding hands with this girl that he says he is in love with.

A mother's intuition... do I trust it?

Response:

I understand your concern. It's one I've heard from more than a few parents when:

— their child asks them a question related to sex

and / or

— when mom or dad (or both) realize that they need to talk about sex with their children.

These parents worry that a discussion about sex could prompt their children to want to "know what sex is about" (i.e., experiment).

Then, in an attempt to deter experimentation, these parents try to steer their preteens and teens in the opposite direction — away from any sexual activity.

They try to do this by saying things like,

"Sex is for grown-ups"

or

"We'll tell you when you're older"

What often happens though, with these types of responses, is one of the following two things, or both:

1. The child's **curiosity** about sex and sexuality increases.

2. The child feels **shame** for having asked a question.

A Better Response in This Type of Situation Would Be for Parents To Be Direct, and to, Tactfully but Candidly Say What They Mean.

Example:

"It's best to wait until you're a responsible adult before having sex."

You could also ask yourself :

"No matter how much I try to shield my son from the subject of sex by not talking about it, he has access to internet, and contact with other kids.

Do I truly think he is clueless about sex?"

If your answer is not a resounding "No," then consider the possibility that kids know quite a bit about sex.

That's why openness is important as parents talk about this subject with their children.

With Tact, Sensitivity, and Candor, Talking About Sex With Your Children Is a Win-Win.

Why?

Because, in my opinion, having this conversation with children

— **Won't** make them **more interested** in sex,

but

— **Will** make it **easier** for them to approach their parents with questions.

Question No. 2 — Setting an Example

Realizing That Being a Good Role-Model Is Not Enough

My daughter is 12. I drive her to school every weekday morning. It's about a 20 to 30 minute drive, depending on traffic.

I enjoy our time together in the car. We chat about all sort of things, or sometimes we'll listen to songs that we both like that are being played on the car radio.

I've started to notice something recently in the way my daughter is behaving in car, because it's a pattern. When we're about a block (two or three minutes) away from her school, she'll ask a question that is in some way related to sex or sexuality.

At that point, there's not enough time for me to respond, so I mostly just listen, or I may say something quick and superficial like,

"That's interesting."

Confession: I'm glad there isn't any time for me to respond. I wouldn't know what to say, or how to say it. I'm uneasy broaching this subject and I find myself thinking:

"I'll discuss it later when the time's right."

Or

"I'm a good role-model... I'm setting a good example for my child about life. So she'll figure it [sex / sexuality] out, as long as I keep being a good role-model." Am I on the right track?

Response:

Yes and No.

The Power of Positive Role-Modeling

It's true that your child learns about life by emulating those around her, so it's natural that as a parent, you would want to be a positive role-model.

So when you [and hopefully your child's father] demonstrate healthy values and habits, this can create a foundation for how your daughter will relate to other people and view the world.

The Risk of...

Misinformation

But....

When it comes to information about sex and sexuality, many of today's kids are being saturated with messages about these subjects from TV, entertainment media, the Internet and peers. The result? They are vulnerable to being misinformed about sex.

I've heard from many parents how concerned they are about the negative role models that tend to saturate our culture, and the detrimental impact that this can have on their children.

The Risk of...

Waiting for "the Right Time"

So, as you (and lots of other parents) are waiting for that perfect moment to have "the talk," or thinking that being a good role-model is sufficient to equip your child with the ability to resist negative influences, take a moment to think about what your child may be experiencing.

Ask yourself:

"While I'm holding off on having "The Talk," is my child at risk for being saturated, or at least being exposed to, messages about sex that puts her at risk to:

— be misinformed

and / or

— Adopt attitudes and beliefs that conflict with what I think about this subject, and would like my child to know?"

If your answer is "YES," to one or both of the questions above, you might want to do an internet search to see how many pregnancies occur annually among minors, and how many cases of of sexually transmitted diseases occur among minors.

Many parents who have done this type of search find that they are alarmed at the results.

Then they tend to ask a question along these lines:

"These numbers are scary. What can be done about this problem?"

My response is generally two-fold:

1. **Resolve any Uneasiness / Discomfort You Feel About Talking About This Sensitive Topic With Your Child.**

2. **Learn How To Talk to Your Child / About Sex in Age-Appropriate Ways.**

For some parents, tackling these two items might mean reaching out for professional help. If you feel that you might be one of those parents, don't hesitate to seek help. Do it for yourself. Do it for your child.

Follow-Up Question Number 1.

Knowing When To Seek Help

I'm comfortable with going to counseling or life coaching if I need it (I've had both in the past).

But I'm not clear if I need it for this, or not.

Maybe I can learn to handle the two items you talk about (resolving discomfort with talking about sex; learning how to talk to my child about sex), on my own.

How do I decide if I need to get extra help with this?

Response:

Sometimes, if people aren't sure if they need counseling or not, they schedule a consultation with a professional to determine whether the service would be beneficial. So that's one way to approach your question.

When My Child Asks Me a Question About Sex, How Do I Respond?

Other parents who were "on the fence" about whether they needed counseling or not, have found it helpful to take a look at **how they respond to their child's questions about sex**... and whether they've been able to:

- **Keep the lines of communication open** with their child,

or whether they

- **Short-circuit the conversation** with their child.

If they did (a) that was a good sign.

If they did (b) then they typically decided that speaking with a counselor would be a good idea.

Follow-Up Question Number 2.

Short-Circuiting the Conversation

Can you give some examples of what parents say if they skip out on (short-circuit) the conversation?

I think it would be helpful for me to see if I do some of that?

Response:

Sure. It's wonderful that you're willing to put your behavior "under the microscope" in this way. Good for you that you're so open.

Keep in Mind That Ideally, Educating Children About Sex Should Be an Ongoing Conversation.

That said, here are some examples of **conversation-stoppers** (i.e., responses from parents that short-circuit addressing their children's questions about sex):

"I'm busy, don't bother me."

"Ask your mother (or father)."

When Children Are Responded To In This Way, It's Not Uncommon For Them To Interpret This Response To Mean,

"I'm Not Supposed To Ask About Sex."

Other responses from parents that **avoid** "the talk" include,

"That's none of your business"

"I don't care what your friends do!"

Follow-Up Question Number 3.

Keeping the Lines of Communication Open

"Can you give some examples of things parents can say in response to a child's questions about sex that keep the lines of communication open?"

Response:

Absolutely.

There are lots of examples. These will vary, depending on:

- The question asked by the child

- The age of the child who is asking the question

And

- The scope of the knowledge that the parent has about sex as it relates to the question being asked

That said, here are two frequently expressed, effective responses that tend to keep "the communication door" open:

"That's a good question"

or

"I'm glad you asked."

Follow-Up Question Number 4.

Handling Being Clueless About the Answer

"What if I genuinely don't know how to answer a question that my child is asking about sexuality, even though I really want to give my child an answer?

I mean, let's say I'm comfortable talking to my child about sex, so there's no issue with that... but I just don't know the answer?"

Response:

If you don't know how to respond to a question, that's really ok.

For starters there are two ways you might approach this situation:

1. You can **offer to find the answer**

Or

2. Depending on your child's age, the **two of you can look it up together**.

Best of luck!

Question No. 3 — Afraid To Talk

Encouraging Teens To Express How They Feel

My wife and I are separated. We live in the same city, so our 14 year old lives with me during the week, and spends weekends and most holidays with her mom.

I wish I could be with her every day, but all things considered, this time-share arrangement is best.

Within the past year or so, my daughter has started to be interested in boys. I'm so happy that she shares this with me. She doesn't say all that much, but she'll drop a quick remark here and there like,

"There's this really cute boy at school"

and

"My backpack was really heavy today and this popular boy offered to carry it for me! My girlfriends were jealous!"

In response to her comments, I don't say much (I don't know what to say, really.) Mostly, I just smile. It's cute to hear these things from her, and I'm happy for her. I'm also happy that she tells me these things.

There's one thing that she said, though, that stuck in my mind... Actually, she said this type of thing twice recently. What happened was that after she told me about the cute boy, she said:

"OMG, I'd never tell mom that, she'd get mad."

And after the shared with me about the popular boy carrying her backpack, she said:

"I can't tell mom about this, she'll yell at me."

I didn't say anything in response to either of these things that my daughter said regarding her mother.

Of course I listened carefully to my daughter as she was talking, and I gave her my 100% attention, but I keep replaying her comments about her mom in my mind.

Now I'm wondering:

Should have responded to my daughter's comments about her mom?

But then I wonder:

If I did respond, what would I say?

Also, I don't to want to talk behind her mom's back. I've heard my friend, who's divorced, badmouth his ex to his child. I know that's not right...I also worry a bit that if I start talking about my child's mom with her, my frustration about our separation might show...

So I feel unclear about two things:

1. Do I need to say anything to my child about what she said about her mom?

2. If yes, what do I say so that it doesn't seem like I'm talking behind her mom's back?

Response:

It's refreshing to hear that the lines of communication are open between you and your daughter. Unfortunately, this is not the case with many father-daughter relationships.

Parents Deserve Praise Too...

So you can feel very good about your parenting regarding the fact that your daughter feels comfortable to share these things with you.

Give yourself a pat on the back, so to speak, and whatever you've been doing to keep the conversation flowing between you and your daughter, **keep doing it!**

Trusting Your Intuition

That said, your intuition — which appears to have been nudging you to address your daughter's comments about her mom — is accurate. I'll explain why in a moment.

But first, you are correct about not wanting to talk about your daughter "behind her mom's back," or to expose your child to your frustrations about the marriage. It's so important that separated (and divorced) parents keep this in mind. Parents must:

Keep Children Out of the Crossfire

This is especially important if spouses (or former spouses) harbor **negativity** (anger, hostility) towards each other about the separation (or divorce.)

Unresolved anger often leads to one parent:

— **Criticizing** the absent parent to their child,

or to

— **Subtle verbal digs** or jabs about the absent parent.

Sometimes unresolved anger manifests **non-verbally**.

Examples:

— Sharp voice tone

— Furrowed brow

— Tapping fingers

— Tapping feet

— Clenched fists

— Fast breathing

— One hand clutches the other hand, elbow or arm

Children are extremely perceptive. They **pick up on verbal and non-verbal cues** that are tell-tale signs of one parent's unresolved anger towards the other parent.

This Puts Children in the Middle of Their Parents' Sore Feelings About Their Failed Relationship.

This is not fair to these children.

Deep down a child's **loyalty** is to **both parents**. So children often experience inner conflict when they feel caught in the middle of one parent's hostility towards the other.

Sometimes a child even feels **guilty** for somehow causing the hostility

"I wish hadn't told dad that I was afraid to talk to mom...!"

This can cause a child to feel depressed. It can also trigger low self-esteem.

Parents Must Put Their Hostility "On Hold."

Although this can be quite a challenge, it is possible for parents who are relating to their child to **"press the pause button"** so to speak, about any **unresolved anger** they may have towards their ex.

This means that co-parents **keep their conflicts to themselves**.

Then, when they talk to their child, they can be:

- **calm**

- **neutral**

and

- **impartial**

instead of

- **resentful**

and / or

- judgemental

Children need to feel like they can confide in their parents.

This is not likely to happen, or not to any great extent, if children expect to get a hostile reaction from one or both parents.

Now, onto your questions:

1. Do I need to say anything to my child about what she said about her mom?

2. If yes, what do I say so that it doesn't seem like I'm talking behind her mom's back?

The answer to your first question is "Yes."

In terms of what to say, you're somewhat limited because your daughter didn't say much. So you don't have much to respond to.

There is still a way to respond to what your daughter shared, though — and before I delve into that response, here's a two-part question that you can ask yourself:

1. Why did my child not say much when she talked about her mom?...

2. Could it be that my child was expecting to get a hostile reaction from me?

If you answered "Yes" to the second part of the question, now's a good time for a

Writing exercise

Fill-in-the-blanks below by finishing the following sentence:

I think my daughter was expecting a hostile reaction to me because

_____

_____

_____

_____

Writing exercise number 2

Fill-in-the-blanks below by finishing the following sentence:

From now on, when my daughter talks about her mother, instead of being hostile (verbally or non-verbally), I will

_____

_____

_____

_____

Now that you've perhaps cracked the door open to, hopefully, more communication with your daughter in the future, let's look at how to handle what she said, as you pointed out in your question:

"OMG, I'd never tell mom that, she'd get mad."

"I can't tell mom about this, she'll yell at me."

There are at least two reasons why a response from you could be appropriate:

1. Since your daughter brought up the issue of her mother potentially getting mad and yelling at her, it is possible that **she wants / needs to talk** about it.

   But she may need **a little nudging** from you before she feels comfortable to share more details.

2. Say, on the off chance, your daughter just made the reference to potentially being the recipient of her mom's anger, **in passing**.

   It's still wise for you, as her parent, to encourage her to talk more about what she said.

Why?

Again, at least two reasons:

- No one (especially a child) likes to be the potential recipient of another person's wrath.

  So it would be wise to **encourage your daughter to express how she feels about this situation**, rather then keep any feelings that she may have about this, buried inside herself.

It's not healthy for anyone, especially children, to suppress emotion inside themselves.

In time, this can lead to all kinds of problems, including intense reactions, depression, disrupted sleep, etc.

- The separation between you and your wife has, no doubt, required (and continues to require) your child to make **huge adjustments** to the fact that **your family is now broken**.

    Your child may have unresolved feelings about this that she has previously pushed down inside herself.

    It would be **unwise to add even more suppressed emotions** that could be added on top of an ever-growing pool of emotions that your daughter has pushed down.

Recap:

Now you have more understanding about:

(a) **Why** your child talked about her mom to you— but not much,

and

(b) **Why** a response from you can be a good idea, nonetheless.

Next, we'll talk about **how** you could respond.

Keep in mind that:

Your child's wellbeing is your priority...

This means that when you respond to her

You set aside any negative feelings that you may have towards your "ex".

Also keep in mind that your child did not share much.

This means that when you respond to her, your objective is to

Encourage your child to express her feelings, and not bottle them up inside.

This also lets your child know that,

She can talk to you comfortably and freely, about anything.

And that

She doesn't need to hold back for fear of being caught in the middle of you and your "ex."

It also means that

Your child is not afraid that sharing her feelings with you will make you sad or maybe, mad.

This is **powerful**, **positive parenting**.

Here's a **script** that you can use to encourage your child to express her feelings.

The script can be used, as-is, or it can be tweaked and / or adapted to the specifics of your situation, if you'd like.

Using a **calm**, **neutral** tone, you could say:

[Your child's name], thank you for sharing your fear of mom getting mad, or being yelled at by her.

Can you share with me a little more about why you feel afraid?

Depending on what / or how much your child says next, you may learn some more **details / background** about the situation.

Regardless of whether you learn more about the situation or not, here's a **general rule** to keep in mind when it comes to asking kids follow-up questions about what they share with you:

Keep your questions brief, simple and to the point.

Don't feel that you need to come up with an answer or some type of fix.

What matters at this point is that,

— Your child says what's on her mind… **fully** and **completely**.

And that

— She begins to realize that she can share **freely** and **openly** with you, **without being judged** or **criticized**.

That is likely to cause her to **feel a lot better**… as if a weight has been lifted off her shoulders, even if, at that point, the two of you didn't talk about or come up with a solution to the problem she was having.

One more thing…

Depending on what your child shares in response to your question about why she feels afraid, a follow-up question could sound something like this:

Thank you for sharing. Can you tell me how that fear feels… how does it feel to be scared like this?

This would invite your child to share on a **deeper** level, as she focuses her answer on the fear itself and **how** that feels, in contrast to telling you **why** she feels afraid (i.e., what are the circumstances that led to her feeling afraid.)

If you don't get to ask the second question as a follow-up to the first one, that's fine. There's no one-size-fits-all way to do this.

Why?

Because every person is unique and so are their circumstances.

But now that you have:

— **More tools in your parenting toolbox**

Along with

— Remembering how much **you love your child**

You can feel

— **More confident** about how to talk to your child about what she told you about her mom

You can also feel

— **More confident** about talking to your child about things that she may choose to share with you **in the future**.

Question No. 4 — Supervision

Balancing Independence and Parental Oversight

Our 16-year-old daughter is a late bloomer. She's dedicated and conscientious about her school work, and for years that was her whole focus.

But since she turned 16 last month, she's been going out more...mostly with her friends from school.

She respects curfews and lets me or her dad know if there's been a change of plans while she's out with her friends, and she checks in with us, and asks if that change is ok.

Her dad and I have no complaints, as far as her developing social life goes, and she continues to get good grades.

My question has to do with a beach party that she went to about a week ago. Actually, it was one of her friend's 16th birthday party.

Her dad and I had met the "birthday girl" before... she's been over to our house when she and my daughter were doing a school project.

So when my daughter said that this friend was having a birthday party that was scheduled for this past Saturday, and she asked her dad and I if she could go, we said, "Yes,"... and we didn't give it another thought.

Looking back at my child's request to go to the party, and after chatting with my sister-in-law who has an 18-year-old son, I should have called the birthday girl's parents and asked some questions to learn more about what they had planned for the party, so my husband and I would be more informed about this event that our daughter would be attending — like who would be at the party, and whether any adults would be attending, as well.

The reason I'm wishing we would have checked out things more before giving our daughter a thumbs up to go to the party, is because after the party was over, we found out something that my daughter did, and this has us worried.

What happened was that on the Sunday morning after the party, my daughter slept in as she often does on Sunday mornings. That was fine.

But the night before, after she came home from the party, she forgot to put her smartphone on the charger in her bedroom, like she usually does. Instead, she left her phone on the kitchen counter,

Now, I never snoop around or go through her room when she's not here, to see what she's been up to.

But on Sunday, when I saw her phone on the kitchen counter, (and I'm not proud of what I'm about to say) I checked her phone to see if there were any photos from the birthday party.

I don't know why I checked. Maybe a mother's instinct?

What I saw shocked me, and also my husband, after I showed him what I saw.

There were about half a dozen selfies where my daughter was standing in suggestive poses, and…

she was wearing a revealing swim suit that I'd never seen her wear before.

I don't know how she got that swimsuit because my husband and I didn't buy it for her — and she doesn't have much money of her own to buy something like that.

It also looks like she posted some of these photos on social media, but I'm not certain.

As of this time, I haven't said anything about this to my daughter.

But my husband and I feel we need to talk to her and find out more about these photos, and also find out more about what happened at the birthday party she went to this past Saturday.

Our problem is that we don't know how to bring this up to our daughter, or what to say...

My husband has a bit of a temper... I'm worried he might be sharp and blunt with our daughter. How do parents handle things like this?

Response:

I appreciate how unsettling this is for you and your husband, and it's good that you're reaching out for some pointers on how to best approach this with your daughter.

Responsible parenting means being involved.

Of course, it wouldn't be wise to sweep this under the rug and look the other way. That wouldn't give you any peace of mind, and it wouldn't be responsible parenting — it's important to get involved so you can get to the bottom of this, and learn

— **What** was going on when those photos were taken,

and

— **Why** those photos were taken.

Responsible parenting means communicating in a calm, clear way.

On the other hand, if your husband "flies off the handle" at your daughter, that would be detrimental… it would most likely close the door to having a positive talk with your daughter about this.

When teens are yelled at, or parents use a sharp (accusatory) tone when "talking" to them, here's what often happens:

- **These children realize that it's not OK to talk to their parents. So they clam up (withdraw, shut down).**

Or

- **A nasty, destructive parent-teen shouting match ensues and nothing positive is accomplished.**

Now, returning to your question:

How do parents handle things like this?

First, you are correct about doing your homework (i.e., calling the birthday girl's parents to find out the details about the party) before telling your daughter she can attend.

It's important that at all times, parents **know** and **approve** of:

— **Where** their children are

— **Who** they are with

and

— **What** they are doing

Some parents think they're being nosey, too "in their child's face", or stifling their child's independence, if they prioritize being up to speed with **Where**, **Who** and **What**.

That's not the case at all. That's responsible parenting. This way, you can be sure that your child is **safe**, in **good company** and having **positive experiences.**

The alternative?

Without parental oversight that is careful, consistent and reasonable, children are at risk for experiencing things that conflict with their parents' values.

Four questions to ask yourself:

1. *"Am I ok with my child being exposed to and influenced by values that conflict with mine?"*

2. *"Whose values do I want my child to learn, adopt and live by? Mine or someone else?"*

3. *"Am I being fair to my child to subject her to having to decide (before she's mature / experienced enough to decide) whose values she should live by ... her mom's or someone else's?"*

Or...

4. *"Am I setting her up to live her best life, if I take an active role in her life and make sure that her experiences (**where** she goes, **who** she's with, **what** she does) are in alignment with my values?"*

If you answered "No" to each of the first three questions, and "Yes" to the fourth question, then keep reading!

Your and your teen have more in common than you might think.

When it comes to talking to your daughter about the photos that you saw on her phone, it's a good idea not to jump right into that topic — if you do, then depending how you approach it, your daughter might feel defensive and shut you out.

Instead, take a step back for a moment, and ask yourself:

"Am I genuinely interested in how the birthday party went?"

"Am I genuinely interested in whether my daughter had a good time at the party?"

If you answered "Yes" to these questions, then you could start the conversation with your daughter by expressing your interest.

If you communicate your interest sincerely, your daughter would probably appreciate your question/s. You have more in common with her than you might be thinking you have, right now

Why?

Because it's natural to **appreciate** and feel **good** when someone is **genuinely expressing interest** in our lives.

We feel **noticed**, we feel **cared about**, we feel like **our life matters** to whomever is asking the question. Your daughter is likely to feel this way, as long as she doesn't get the sense that you are:

- Quizzing her

- Interrogating her

Or that

- She's done something wrong

Or that

- You have an ulterior motive

Even if you had not found the photos, and even if you did not, therefore, have a need to talk to your teen about the photos, it would be healthy to ask your teen about the party (preferably when she came home from the party, or the next morning.)

Either way, you could start the conversation with a simple question or two, like:

"[Insert teen's name) how did the birthday party go? Did you have a good time?"

Depending on your teen's responses, you might have some follow-up questions. If feasible, your follow-up questions might include:

"Was [insert birthday girl's name] mom or dad at the party?"

"Were there any other adults at the party?"

"Were there any boys at the party?"

Your daughter's responses to the first two questions would help you to determine if **a supervising adult** was present at the party. (This is something you would have found out, by calling the birthday girl's parents ahead of the party.)

The reason for asking the third question is to determine whether your daughter was striking those suggestive poses that you saw in the photos, to impress boys.

Of course, you could just come right out and ask her these questions when you get to the part of your conversation with her where you talk about the photos.

Keep "the talk" relaxed and flowing.

But…if you can gather this information in a more informal way, by expressing curiosity about how the party went, that's more likely to keep the conversation **relaxed** and **flowing**.

Feeling guilty about "snooping".

So now it's time to ask your daughter about the photos. If you're like a lot of parents I've talked to, you probably don't want to tell her that you were snooping because you feel guilty for doing that.

To the contrary: It appears that your intention was sound — a part of you ("mother's instinct?") felt this "research" was necessary to keep your daughter out of harm's way.

Just because your child is a good student and has given you no reason (up until now) to question her behavior, the fact remains… she's 16 and inexperienced.

It would be unwise to assume that your teen is immune to peer pressure or possibly acting immaturely because she's curious.

So consider trusting the "mother's instinct" and keeping in mind that **it is not your nature to be a "snooper,"** but that there are times when parents need to **monitor** their children's activities more vigilantly to keep them **safe**.

That said, ideally both you and your husband will be present when this talk with your daughter occurs. Either one of you could initiate this talk, but since you "discovered" the photos (and he has "a bit of a temper"), you might consider leading the conversation.

In that case, being honest and factual can't steer you wrong. You might say something like:

"[Insert child's name] I'm so happy you enjoyed the party.

I need to tell you something...

You know I don't go through other people's things — and your dad and I have taught you not to do that either.

But on Saturday, I saw your phone in the kitchen, and I looked at the party photos you took.

I feel bad for looking, and I apologize to you for that, but something prompted me to do it... a mother's instinct maybe.

Anyway, I was surprised to see the photos, and I felt your dad needed to see them.

We're not mad at you... and you're not in trouble, but we don't know what to make of those photos.

Can you tell us about the photos?... Like,

***Why** you took them?*

***Where** you got that bathing suit?*

and

*— **Who** was there when you took the photos?*

and

*— **Anything else** you'd like to tell us?"*

Follow-Up Question Number 1.

Teaching Teens Self-Respect

My fear is that my daughter will say that she did post the photos on social media, and that there were boys at the party who watched her take the photos, and urged her to post them on social media.

If that happens, I think my husband will leave the room because he knows that if he stays in the room, he will "hit the roof."

So it will be up to me to finish talking to my daughter. Even though she's a really good daughter, and we've taught her good values and morals, I've never talked to her about this subject before... we've never had to deal with this.

How do I encourage her not to show off her body in front of her peers like she did in the photos (even though she's very pretty and has a lovely body), and not to post it on the internet for the world to see?

Response:

Curiosity about sexuality typically escalates during the preteen years. This is because physical changes tend to stimulate various feelings, including attraction and arousal. Since your daughter is "a late bloomer," it's possible she's experiencing an escalation in her curiosity.

It sounds like you're wanting to encourage your daughter to **respect herself** and **her body**. This means that even though she has a lovely body, she doesn't need to show it off in order to be popular.

Create teachable moments.

Parents have found it useful to use what happens around them as a conversation opener or "teachable moment," as I like to call it.

For example, if there's a TV program, a magazine, or music video that your daughter enjoys, you might make reference to an outfit that a TV star is wearing, or a model in a magazine, or an artist in the music video, to show how that depicts sexuality.

Based on what they see in the mass-media, pre-teens (and late-blooming teens, such as your daughter) can be especially vulnerable to thinking that "sex appeal" is something they must develop to be popular and attract a boyfriend or girlfriend.

You might open the conversation by asking what your daughter what she thinks of a skimpy outfit that she sees someone wearing.

Listen without overreacting or judging.

Then your daughter is more likely to listen when you start talking.

Assure your teen that it's ok to say "No."

Emphasize **self-worth**. Self-respecting teens are not likely to flaunt their bodies so that they will be liked.

Self-respecting teens have the confidence and integrity to say "No" to peer pressure and making poor choices so that they will be liked.

Explain that healthy relationships are based on **getting to know someone**... their **character** and **values**, for example**,** and that not all contact with a boyfriend or girlfriend must be sexual.

There are lots of ways to express affection - intimate talks, long walks, holding hands.

Teens often push the limits.

Even though you have taught your daughter good values and morals, it's not uncommon for teens to push the limits.

Most teens know right from wrong. What can happen though, is that their curiously can cause them to take risks that seem out of character (e.g., your daughter posing for suggestive selfies).

One reason teens behave this way is because they like the excitement of seeing if they can do something and not get caught.

Misdirected curiosity can get teens into trouble.

Follow-Up Question Number 2.

Taking preventative steps

I worry that because socializing with other teens is so new to my daughter, there may be more "surprises" (like the out-of-character photos she took) on the way.

So, after we have this talk with her, how can we keep an eye on her to be sure she doesn't make bad choices?

We don't want to stifle her, and we want to support her independence, but this photo episode makes me think that I (and also her father) would feel a little more at ease if we could keep a bit of a closer eye on her.

Response:

Be sure to continue to keep the **lines of communication open**.

Keep a balance between:

— Letting your daughter know **how proud you are of her**, and assuring her that **you believe in her.**

While at the same time

— Explaining to her that because she's entering into some new, **uncharted territory in her life** (i.e., socializing),

That means

— You're going to be more involved (at least right now), to help make sure that she **doesn't get off track**.

Helping Your Teen Make Positive Choices.

Here are some ways that you can begin to be a **positive influence** on the choices that your teen makes.

Always **know** and **approve** of

— **Where** your child is,

— **Who** she is with

And

— **What** she is doing.

Be **mindful** of what your child is:

— **Reading,**

— **Listening** to,

— **Watching**

And

— **Doing online.**

For more about monitoring your teen's online activity, read my article, *3 Ways to Stop Your Teen From Making Risky Choices*, published on The Huffington Post

https://bit.ly/2wa5yhO

In addition,

— When a friend is **visiting** your child at your home, and they're "hanging out" in your child's bedroom — and sexual activity is a possibility, keep your child's **bedroom door open**.

And

— Set **reasonable rules**. Rules that are too restrictive tend to invite rebellion.

— If a **rule is broken**, apply a **fair, reasonable** consequences with **consistency**. Otherwise your child won't take the rules seriously.

WHAT'S NEXT?

Resources... To Keep Navigating the Teen Years With Confidence

I hope you've enjoyed this Life Guide. It is "technically" complete, but I wanted to give you some **more resources on parenting** (so you can not only survive the teen years, but thrive) **and self-care** (part of being a great parent is taking great care of yourself) ... in case you'd like to continue the learning and the growing with me.

Here are some of my favorites — articles I've authored,[3] books I've written, and inspiring insights I shared when I was interviewed by a reporter from the Weekend Today Show, to savor at your leisure.

Enjoy...

---

[3] All articles referenced in this section were published online.

PARENTING

3 Ways to Stop Your Teen From Making Risky Choices
— Published on The Huffington Post

http://www.huffingtonpost.com/dr-suzanne-gelb/3-ways-to-stop-your-teen-from-making-risky-choices-about-dating-and-sex_b_5925602.html

7 Dangerous Lessons We Need To Stop Teaching Our Kids
— Published on Mind Body Green

https://www.mindbodygreen.com/0-14586/7-dangerous-lessons-we-need-to-stop-teaching-our-kids.html

It Starts With You. How To Raise Happy, Successful Children By Being The Best Role Model You Can Possibly Be — A Guidebook, by Dr. Gelb

https://www.amazon.com/Starts-You-Successful-Becoming-Guidebook/dp/0692647392/ref=tmm_pap_swatch_0?_encoding=UTF8&qid=1553581148&sr=1-4

How to Get your Kids to Cooperate: And Help Them Become the BEST Grown-Ups They Can Be (A Life Guide)

https://amzn.to/2V4AzxD

Praise for Dr. Gelb's Life Guides

"Dr. Gelb has a gentle spirit that instantly makes you feel like you've come home. The depth of her wisdom is undeniable, her curiosity is insatiable and her love is palpable. These qualities

make her the perfect guide for life. In the pages of the Life Guides you will find practical and proven processes to support you in living your great life. Whether it's heart-centered wisdom on navigating the dating world, love-based strategies for becoming a parent, or reaching your ideal weight through kindness, Dr. Gelb's Life Guides are gifts to be treasured."

— Dr. Gemma Stone, Psychologist, Mentor, Author

Three Lessons You Must Teach Your Kids. (The sooner the better. But it's never too late)

— Published on my column "All Grown Up" on Psychology Today
https://www.psychologytoday.com/us/blog/all-grown/201503/parents-three-lessons-you-must-teach-your-kids

Good Parenting Isn't Complicated — Here's Why

—Originally Published on Maria Shriver; soon to be published on my column "All Grown Up" on Psychology Today

bit.ly/1QlQQsE

Spring Cleaning for Your Life [Part 1/3]
— Published on The Huffington Post

https://www.huffpost.com/entry/spring-cleaning-for-your_n_7253908

When the Other Parent Doesn't Play Fair
— Published in Family Advocate, Vol. 30, No. 1 (Summer 2007) American Bar Association

bit.ly/1QmYYpq

Raising an Organized Child In a Blended Family
— Published in Family Advocate, Vol. 36, No. 1 (Summer 2013) American Bar Association

https://bit.ly/2HJgxFW

SELF-CARE

6 Self-Sabotaging Habits You Need To Drop Right Now
— Published on Mind Body Green.

https://www.mindbodygreen.com/0-14014/6-selfsabotaging-habits-you-need-to-drop-right-now.html

Stressed Out at Work? How to Cope -- Without Turning to Food or Booze
— Published on The Huffington Post.

https://www.huffpost.com/entry/stressed-out-at-work-how_n_6711034

The Greatest Cheerleader One Can Have — Lives Within: How To Stay Strong When Not Everyone Is Cheering for our Success.
— Published in Dr. Gelb's column, "All Grown Up" on Psychology Today

https://www.psychologytoday.com/us/blog/all-grown/201902/the-greatest-cheerleader-person-can-have-lives-within

Why Accomplishment Often Leaves Us Feeling "Empty." How to heal that longing, at last.
— Published in Dr. Gelb's column, "All Grown Up" on Psychology Today

https://www.psychologytoday.com/us/blog/all-grown/201905/why-accomplishment-often-leaves-us-feeling-empty

How To Reach Your Ideal Weight: Through Kindness Not Craziness (A Life Guide)

https://amzn.to/2JMqRyi

Praise for Dr. Gelb's Life Guides

"Learning how to love yourself and treat yourself kindly — even when your life, career, body, and relationships aren't 'totally perfect' — is one of the hardest things to do. Dr. Suzanne Gelb breaks down the art of self-love into practical steps. No woo-woo vagueness. Just easy-to-follow exercises pulled from her 28-year career in the field. If you're looking for practicality and effectiveness, these Life Guides are a steal of a deal."

—Susan Hyatt, Master Certified Life Coach, Published Author

"This Life Guide came at the perfect time. My two fears about losing weight were dispelled immediately and it was such a relief to know that I can start looking after myself without the worry of going to the gym or going on another desperate diet.

The audio helped re-frame the reasons why I've let my weight spiral out of control and the work book helped me set out an action plan. Thanks, Dr. Gelb, for your Life Guide, here's to a happier, healthier life."

—Amanda Herbert, photographer

If You Want to Make Tomorrow Less Stressful—Start Tonight
— Published in Dr. Gelb's column, "Be Well At Work," on The Muse

https://www.themuse.com/advice/if-you-want-to-make-tomorrow-less-stressfulstart-tonight

Side note: The Muse is an online platform that attracts more than 75 million people each year, to help them be at the top of their game at work.

I'm honored to have received the praise below, from Adrian Granzella Larssen, Editor-in-Chief, in response to an article that I wrote for The Muse:

"Wow! This is fantastic stuff. You're clearly incredible at what you do, and I'm so thrilled to share your advice with our audience!"

You Are The Best Investment You'll Ever Make
— Published on my column, "All Grown Up," on Psychology Today.

https://www.psychologytoday.com/blog/all-grown/201511/you-are-the-best-investment-youll-ever-make

Why Positive Affirmations Don't Always Work (And What Does)
— Published on Tiny Buddah

http://tinybuddha.com/blog/why-positive-affirmations-dont-always-work-and-what-does/

How to Succeed Everywhere: 10 Tips for Balance at Work, Home, in Relationships
— Written by Shelby Marra, published online on NBC's Today.

https://www.today.com/health/how-become-high-achieving-woman-work-your-relationship-parent-t33071

Side note: As my colleague, friend, and gifted writing teacher, Alex Franzen said: *"THIS IS AMAZING! Being interviewed by a reporter from NBC's Today Show? Uh, that's the big leagues!"*

Yes, that's what happened. Shelby Marra with NBC's Today Show in New York, requested an interview with me so that she could write this article featuring me, for TODAY.com's Successful Women series.

How Successful People Do More in 24 Hours Than the Rest of Us Do in a Week
— Published on Newsweek; also published on my column, "Be Well At Work," on The Muse

https://www.newsweek.com/career/how-successful-people-do-more-24-hours-rest-us-do-week

The Love Tune-Up: How to Amp Up the Love That's Naturally Inside You to Enjoy Happy, Healthy Relationships. (A self-paced, 14-day course.)

https://amzn.to/2UzTSP6

The Life Guide on How to Care for Yourself When You're a Caregiver for Somebody Else.

http://drsuzannegelb.com/life-guide-care-for-yourself-caregiver/

Praise

I enjoyed your Caregivers Guide. It is appealing, well-organized and has great information.

—Dr. Mary Clark, PhD, psychologist

Dr. Gelb's "How to Care for Yourself Life Guide" is brilliant, helpful and so necessary.

Having myself been a caretaker four times, I can tell you that the last thing someone needs is one more overwhelming thing to do. You are already operating in a complete state of overwhelm and yet still need some support and an outlet.

Suzanne has created the perfect easy, but powerful. way to do something for yourself. The question prompts with fill-in-the-blanks, makes doing the work feel like a pleasurable outlet. Through her questions and suggestions it's as if she's walking along side you gently guiding you with her big, open, nonjudgemental heart.

If you are feeling the need for something supportive, but feel like you can't deal with even one more thing, this guide is a super gentle, but powerful way, might just be the answer.

—Tracy Baum-Finkel

Before, self-care wasn't a word I ever would have used — it felt selfish and indulgent... but after working through this guide, I see how easily I can make myself feel better — and how that helps me take better care of my loved ones.

I absolutely loved how this guide broke everything down, step by step. I never felt overwhelmed.

—Rebecca Rapple

ABOUT THE AUTHOR

Dr. Suzanne Gelb, Ph.D., J.D. is a psychologist, life coach, TV commentator and author.

Dr. Gelb's inspiring insights on personal growth have been featured on more than 200 radio programs, 200 TV interviews, and online on Time, Newsweek, Forbes, The Huffington Post, NBC's Today, Psychology Today, Positively Positive, The Muse and many other places, as well.

Dr. Gelb served as a parenting expert writer for Hawaii Parent magazine for over 14 years and appeared regularly on television to share tips on a parenting segment for 6 years.

Dr. Gelb's powerful article **Three Ways to Stop Your Teen From Making Risky Choices About Dating and Sex**, was published on The Huffington Post. She also wrote, **7 Dangerous Lessons We Need To Stop Teaching Our Kids,** published on Mind Body Green. As a contributing writer to *Psychology Today* with a regular column, "All Grown Up," Dr. Gelb's articles on parenting include, **10 Ways to Become the Parent Your Children Really Need**.

Dr. Gelb believes that it is never too late to become the person — and parent — you want to be. Strong. Confident. Calm. Creative. Free of all of the burdens that have held you back — no matter what has happened in the past.

To learn more, visit DrSuzanneGelb.com.

OTHER BOOKS BY THE AUTHOR

It Starts With You – How to Raise Happy, Successful Children by Becoming the Best Role-Model You Can Possibly Be. A Guidebook For Parents.

How to Get Your Kids to Cooperate and Help Them Become the Best Grown-Ups They Can Be. (A Life Guide.)

How to Get Ready to Be a Parent and Be the Best Mom or Dad You Can Possibly Be. (A Life Guide.)

How to Forgive the One Who Hurt You Most. (A Life Guide.)

How to Deal With People Who Drive You Absolutely Nuts. (A Life Guide.)

Aging With Grace, Strength and Self-Love. (A Life Guide.)

How to Navigate Being Single and Savor Your Dating Adventure. (A Life Guide.)

The Love Tune-Up: How to Amp Up the Love That's Naturally Inside You to Enjoy Happy, Healthy Relationships.

How to Rekindle That Spark and Create the Relationship and Sex Life That You Want. (A Life Guide.)

How to Find Work That You Love When You're Stuck in a Job That You Hate. (A Life Guide.)

How to Reach Your Ideal Weight Through Kindness, Not Craziness. (A Life Guide.)

Welcome Home: Release Addictions and Return to Love.

How to Care for Yourself When You're a Caregiver for Somebody Else. (A Life Guide.)

Real Men Don't Vacuum. And Other Misguided Myths That Cause Conflict in Relationships.

INDEX[4]

A

age appropriate, 3, 5, 18, 36, 49
apologize(ing), 14, 26, 79

B

bend-the-rules, 11, 21

C

clam up, 73
confide, 62
confidence, 81, 85
confident, 69, 94
consequences, 4, 12, 13, 18, 19, 21, 32, 37, 84
consistency, 84
criticizing the absent parent, 60
curiosity, 7, 25, 40, 44, 78, 80, 82, 86
curious, 7, 31, 36, 78

D

dating and sex, 1, 2, 3, 5, 31, 36, 86

deter, 14, 44
difficult, 3, 25, 36
divorce/separated, 57, 58, 59

E

educate, 18, 19, 29, 41
education, 28, 30
emotional health risks of sex, 28
enforce consequences, 11, 12
enforcing consequences, 4, 21, 32, 37

G

good role-model, 46, 48
grounded, 12, 13
grow out of it, 39, 40
guidelines, 2, 18
guilty, 2, 61, 78

H

harsh, 4, 14
healthy choices, 1, 2, 3, 5

---

[4] The page numbers in this index refer to the printed version of this book.

hormones, 7, 25, 39, 40
"hypocrisy radar", 32

I

ignorance, 40
in love, 39, 40, 41, 43
influence, 3, 7, 18, 83
internet, 7, 15, 30, 44, 47, 48, 80
intimacy, 1, 2, 40
intuition, 43, 59

J

just a phase, 39
"just too late", 36

L

last chance guidebook, 3
lead(ing) by example, 33, 34, 35
lines of communication, 51, 54, 59, 83
listen(ed), 2, 29, 46, 58, 81
loneliness, 25, 27
low self-esteem, 25, 61

M

misinformation, 47
model(ing), 3, 32, 37, 48

mother's instinct, 71, 78, 79

N

navigating the teen years, 85
negative influences, 48
negativity, 59

O

ongoing conversation, 53
online dating (sites), 18, 19
online safety, 17
options, 15, 21, 22

P

parent-approved options, 21
parenting, 59, 67, 73, 74, 85, 86, 87, 94
parenting challenges, 38
parenting tool box, 69
peer pressure, 7, 25, 27, 40, 78, 81
physical health risks of sex, 28
poor decision-making, 40
positive choices, 83
positive social experiences, 7
powerful, positive parenting, 67
professional help, 35, 49
push the limits, 82

R

reinforcing clear boundaries, 23
resist conforming, 21
resist negative influences, 48
risky sexual behavior, 4
role-model(ing), 46, 47, 86, 95
rules, 4, 11, 13, 14, 15, 18, 19, 21, 32, 36, 84

S

safety practice(s), 3, 4, 5, 6, 12, 17, 21, 24, 29, 32, 33
say(ing) "No", 23, 24, 25, 26, 27, 81
seek help, 35, 49, 50
self-respect(ing), 22, 25, 27, 49, 80, 81
separation, 58, 59, 65
setting rules, 4, 21, 32, 36
sex education, 28
sexually transmitted diseases, 48
shame, 44
site-blocking, 19
sneaking out, 12
snoop(ing), 71, 78
social media, 19, 72, 80
sound morals, 22
supervise (dating), 6, 7, 8, 9, 13, 18, 19, 22, 27
supervising adult, 77
suppress emotion, 65

T

taking preventative steps, 82
talk about sex, 2, 27, 29, 31, 39, 41, 43, 44, 45, 48, 49, 50, 53, 56, 80
the media, 7, 19, 47, 72, 80, 81
the power of "No", 24, 28, 37
"The Talk", 29, 43, 48
too late, 2, 3, 36, 87, 94
tools, 19, 30, 38, 69
typical questions, 38

U

unplanned pregnancy, 10
unresolved anger, 59, 60, 61

V

verbal and non-verbal cues, 60

W

ways to express affection, 26, 82
well-adjusted (life), 1, 4, 37, 38
where, who, and what, 74
worried, 1, 24, 71, 72
writing exercise, 63

www.ingramcontent.com/pod-product-compliance
Lightning Source LLC
Chambersburg PA
CBHW030059100526
44591CB00008B/203